MOM, DAD, WHAT DOES IT MEAN TO BE JEWISH?

LEARNING THE BASICS OF JUDAISM WHILE HAVING FUN!

SHAUL GAVRIEL

COPYRIGHT © 2023 SHAUL GAVRIEL
© LUMIÈRE HEBRAÏQUE EDITION
ALL RIGHTS RESERVED.
ISBN: 9798862187069

Dear Parents,

Thank you for choosing our book **'Mom, Dad, What's It Like to Be Jewish? - Learn the Basics of Judaism While Having Fun!'** for your children. We understand the importance of teaching our children the values and traditions that are close to our hearts, and that's why this book has been carefully crafted to assist you in this endeavor.

This book is written with the aim of making **Judaism accessible** and **understandable** for children aged 6 to 12. Throughout these pages, we explore the history of Judaism, its practices, its values, and we offer a range of games and activities to make this learning both fun and interactive. A simple glossary of Judaism-specific vocabulary is provided to help clarify terms that may be new to your children.

Our goal is not only to **impart** the **basics** of **Judaism** but also to **promote universal values** such as respect, justice, and peace. We hope that through this book, your children will develop a deep understanding and love for their cultural and spiritual heritage while learning the importance of these values in their everyday lives.

Your **opinion matters greatly** to us. If you've found this book helpful and think it could benefit other families, we would be extremely grateful if you could take a moment to leave a review on our Amazon sales page. Your feedback not only helps us improve our work but also assists other parents in making an informed choice.

Thank you again for choosing our book to accompany your children's education. We hope it will be a source of joy, discovery, and learning for them.

Best wishes,

Shaul GAVRIEL

Find us by **scanning** this **QR Code:**

This book belongs to:

....

Offered by:

....

CONTENTS

1 INTRODUCTION — 9

2 THE HISTORY OF JUDAISM — 10
- The origines of Judaism — 10
- Great Figures in Jewish History — 14
- Exile and Dispersion of the Jewish — 18
- The Return to the Land of Israel — 21

3 JEWISH PRACTICES — 23
- Jewish Holidays — 23
- Sabbath and its Rituals — 27
- Kosher Food — 31
- Prayer and Synagogues — 34

4 JEWISH VALUES — 37
- The Importance of Study and Learning — 37
- Charity and Kindness Toward Others — 40
- Respecting Parents and Elders — 42
- Justice and Peace in the World — 44

5 GAMES & ACTIVITIES — 46
- Games — 46
- Solutions — 65
- Activities — 67

6 GLOSSARY — 68

INTRODUCTION

Hello, young explorer!

Today, we're setting off on an incredible adventure, and do you know where we're headed? The wonderful world of Judaism!

What is a Jew? What does it mean to be Jewish... That's an excellent question, and it's precisely the mystery we're going to solve together throughout this book.

Being Jewish, you'll see, is a fascinating blend of **religion**, **traditions**, **history**, and a **very special way of life**. Together, we'll travel through time, meet extraordinary characters, and discover customs and holidays that, I promise you, are truly unique!

Being Jewish means belonging to a great people, a large family, with Judaism as their religion. In this book, we're going to explore the fundamentals of Judaism together.

Get ready to have fun because this book is full of games, puzzles, and quizzes to make our journey even more exciting!

So, are you ready to dive into the adventure?

THE HISTORY OF JUDAISM

The Origins of Judaism

A very, very long time ago, nearly 4,000 years back, in a farway land, a man named **Abraham** lived in a city called Ur (Mesopotamia). Abraham was an **extraordinary** man. While everyone else around him worshiped multiple gods, Abraham had a different idea. He believed in a **single**, **powerful entity** that had shaped every mountain, stream, and star in the endless sky. This entity was God. So, Abraham was a **monotheist**, meaning someone who believes in just one God.

One day, as the sky began to tint with the soft colors of dawn, a voice thundered in the air, a voice that seemed to come from everywhere and nowhere at the same time. It was **God**, speaking directly to **Abraham**. God told him to leave his cozy home in Ur, to leave his native land, and to set off for a distant land, a land flowing with milk and honey, a land called **Canaan**. This is the land we now know as **Israel**.

God made a promise to Abraham. He told him he would be the father of a **great nation**, a nation that would worship God and be a beacon for all other nations in the world. Despite the uncertainty and fear, Abraham **trusted God**. He gathered his family and belongings, and set off for Canaan, thereby starting the wondrous and sometimes tumultuous history of the Jewish people.

Over the centuries, the **descendants of Abraham**, who would become the **Jewish people**, faced numerous challenges. They were enslaved by the mighty Pharaoh of Egypt, who forced them to labor hard under the scorching sun to build his grand monuments. But even in these difficult times, they **never forgot their faith in God**.

Then came another challenge. The **Babylonians**, a powerful empire of the time, invaded their land and **destroyed** their **sacred temple** in **Jerusalem**. The Jews were taken far from their homes into exile in Babylon. But even far away, even facing pain and loss, they held on. They continued to **practice their faith**, sing their songs, and tell their stories, thus preserving their **unique identity** and rich culture.

Over the centuries, **Judaism evolved** and developed in fascinating ways. Two texts have been particularly significant in this evolution. The **first** is the **Torah**, the sacred book of Judaism, considered the **word of God** Himself. The Torah contains **laws**, **stories**, and **teachings** that guide the lives of Jews.

The **second** significant **text** is the **Talmud**. The Talmud is a collection of **discussions**, **arguments**, and **interpretations** surrounding the Torah. It was written by learned rabbis who sought to deeply **understand** how to apply the teachings of the **Torah** in everyday life.

And so, this is the **story** of **Judaism**, a story that spans **thousands of years**, crossing continents, empires, and eras. It's a story of **untamed faith**, **unwavering courage**, and **perseverance** against adversity. It's a **story of celebrating life** and **learning divine teachings**.

Are you ready to **dive deeper** into this fascniating **adventure**?

Then let's go, for there's so much more to discover about this incredible story!

Great Figures in Jewish History

After getting acquainted with **Abraham** in the previous chapter, it's time to meet three other significant figures: **Moses**, King David, and Queen Esther. Their stories are the precious threads that weave the rich tapestry of **Jewish history**.

First, there is **Moses**, a man who grew up in the luxury of Pharaoh's palace in Egypt but never forgot that he was a **child of Israel**. His life took an extraordinary turn when he decided to stand **against** the **injustice** done to **his people**. Guided by **God**, Moses succeeded in **freeing** the Israelites from Egyptian slavery.

But **Moses** story doesn't end there. Imagine crossing a barren desert, overcoming countless obstacles, and even parting a sea! Moses did all this. And at the end of this exhausting journey, he received the **Ten Commandments** from **God** atop Mount Sinai. These commandments established **life rules** to help people live in **harmony** and mutual **respect**.

Next comes **King David**, a simple shepherd who won the hearts of an entire nation. He proved his **bravery** when called upon to **face** a formidable giant named **Goliath**. Armed only with his **sling** and **unwavering faith**, David **triumphed** over the foe, showing that greatness lies not in size but in the **heart**.

David became a **great king**, and under his rule, **Jerusalem thrived**. But he was not just a king and a warrior; he was also a **great poet**. His psalms are lyrical poems filled with emotions, hope, and faith in God. These words, written thousands of years ago, are still whispered and sung today.

Lastly, we meet Queen **Esther**. She was a simple **Jewish girl** living in Persia. Her life changed when she became queen to King Ahasuerus. When the wicked Haman, advisor to the king, prepared a decree to eliminate all Jews, Esther displayed **great courage**. She risked her **life** to save her **people**. At a banquet, Esther revealed her true Jewish identity to the king and denounced Haman. The king overturned the decree and punished Haman. Thanks to her **bravery**, Esther **saved** her **people**. She reminds us that **faith** and **courage** can help us overcome any **challenge**.

These three figures, **Moses**, **David**, and **Esther**, with their courage, determination, and faith, are role models for all Jewish children. They show that it is possible to overcome obstacles, to fight for what is **right**, and to make a **difference** in the world.

Now, let these stories **resonate within you, soak in the lessons** they teach. And **get ready**, for our journey through the history of Judaism is far from over. In the following pages, we will explore even more captivating and instructive moments of this **fascinating story**.

Exile and Dispersion of the Jewish People

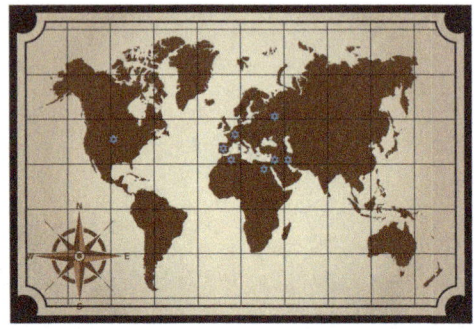

Here we are now at an important **turning** point in our **story**, that of the **exile** and **dispersion** of the Jewish people. Do you know what exile is? It's when you're **forced to leave** your home, your country, and you can't return. Dispersion is when a **people** are spread out in **several different places**, kind of like when you throw flower seeds into the wind and they land everywhere.

The **Jewish people** experienced this after the destruction of the Second Temple of Jerusalem in 70 AD by the Romans. Imagine the broken hearts of the Jews, forced to **leave** the place they loved so much and **scattered across** the vast **Roman Empire**. This was the beginning of a very difficult period that lasted for **centuries**.

18

Over the years, Jews were forced to **leave** many **places** to escape people who **disliked** them just because they were Jewish. They found new homes in Egypt, Babylon, Syria, and Persia. But even there, they were often persecuted, especially under the Persian empire, where they were not **allowed** to **practice** their **religion**.

During the Middle Ages, Jews settled in **Western Europe** and **North Africa**. They were welcomed by local communities, but again, it didn't last. Jews were often **expelled** and **persecuted**, as happened in **Spain** in **1492** during the Reconquista.

In the 18th century, some Jews began to settle in **North America** and **Russia**, where they could freely practice their religion. But that did not stop the persecution of Jews, especially in Eastern Europe, where they suffered **terrible violence** called **pogroms**.

The **worst persecution** the Jewish people have ever suffered occurred during **World War II**. It's a **dark period** called the **Holocaust**, where millions of Jews lost their lives due to the **cruelty** of the Nazis.

But despite all these **trials**, the Jewish people have shown **great strength**. They have always held on, keeping their **faith** and **culture** very much alive. They have shown that even in the toughest moments, it is possible to **survive** and **thrive**. And that's a message of **hope** we can all take to heart.

The Return to the Land of Israel

As you now know, the Jewish people have **lived all over** the **world** for centuries. That's because they were kicked out of their home, the **Holy Land**, by mean and war-loving people. But they never forgot their original home, **Israel**.

The movement to go **back to Israel** is called **Aliyah**. In the **19th century**, lots of Jewish people started coming back to **Palestine**, which was part of the big Ottoman Empire back then. They **worked really hard** to **build** new **towns** and farming communities.

In this new land, Jewish people rolled up their sleeves to build homes, farms, and even entire towns. They planted trees, grew fields, and raised animals. During the awful World War II, **many Jewish people** in Europe **had to leave** their homes and many c**ame to Palestine**. The movement to **return** got even **stronger**.

In **1947**, a very important group called the **United Nations** decided to make a **country** for the **Jewish people**. They also decided to make a country for the Arab people, both in Palestine. On **May 14**, **1948**, the **State of Israel** was **officially made**. It was a **very happy day** for **Jewish people** everywhere.

Today, **Israel** is a **lively** country with people from many **different places**. The Land of Israel is still a very special place for Jewish people all around the world. Many come to **visit** historic spots and some even choose to **live there**.

JEWISH PRACTICES

Jewish Holidays

Jewish **holidays** are **big deals** for Jewish people all around the world, like stars in the sky of the year. They shine all by themselves, **reminding** us of important moments in Jewish **history**, valuable lessons, and times to get **together** with **family** and **friends**. Each holiday is like a window into a world of **traditions** and **teachings** that go back thousands of years.

First up is **Passover**, the holiday that **reminds** us how the Jewish people were **freed** from **slavery** in Egypt. Passover lasts **eight days** and starts with a special dinner called the **Seder**. At the Seder, we tell the story of leaving Egypt and eat foods that mean **something special**. One of these foods is **matzah**, a flatbread that reminds us how the Jews had to leave Egypt so quickly they didn't have time for their bread to rise. But Passover isn't just a meal; it's also a time to clean the house to make it "**kosher for Passover**", meaning no yeast allowed. By doing this, we **remember** our ancestors' journey and become part of their **story**.

Next, we have **Shavuot**, the holiday that **celebrates** when the Jews **got** the **Torah** on Mount Sinai. For Shavuot, it's **traditional** to stay up all **night studying** the Torah. Imagine that, staying awake all night to **read stories** and **teachings** that are super old! And the **next day**, we go to the **synagogue** to **hear** the **Ten Commandments** being read. It's a **strong reminder** of how **important** the **Torah** is in Jewish **life**.

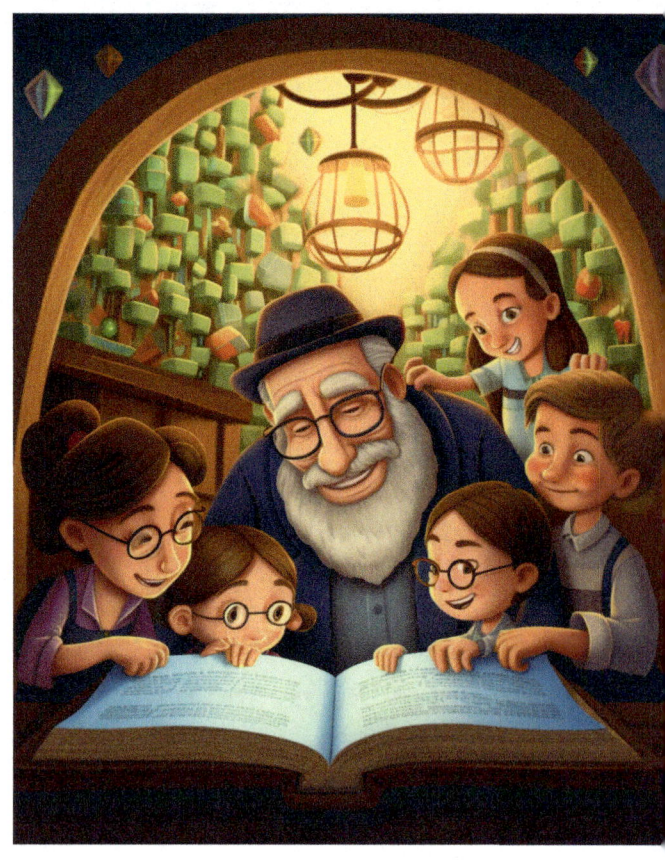

Then comes **Rosh Hashanah**, the **Jewish New Year**. It's a time for **reflection** and **repentance**, a moment to look back on the **past year** and make plans for the **year ahead**. During Rosh Hashanah, we blow the **shofar**, a ram's horn, like an **alarm clock** calling us to be the **best version** of ourselves. This holiday is also an opportunity to savor **symbolic** foods that evoke our **history** and **hopes** for the future, such as an apple dipped in honey to wish for a sweet year, and a pomegranate that symbolizes abundance.

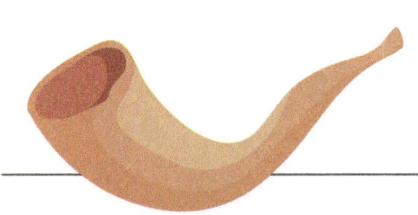

Next, ten days later, we celebrate **Yom Kippur**, the **Day of Atonement**. It's a day when we **fast** and **pray** to say **sorry** for any **mistakes**. It's a day to **think** deep thoughts, but it's also a freeing day because, in the end, we hope to be **forgiven** and start the new year with a **clean slate**.

Right after Yom Kippur, we celebrate **Sukkot**, a **happy holiday** that reminds us how **God** kept the **Jews safe** during their desert journey after leaving Egypt. During Sukkot, we **build** a little hut called a **sukkah** where we **eat** and **celebrate**. It's a way to remember our **history** and get closer to **nature**.

Finally, in the **middle** of **winter**, we celebrate **Hanukkah**, the Festival of **Lights**. This holiday remembers the Maccabees' win against the Greeks and taking back the Temple in Jerusalem. **Each evening** for **eight days**, we light one more **candle** on the **menorah** to remember the miracle of the oil jar that lasted eight days instead of one.

Each Jewish **holiday** is a unique **adventure**, full of **history**, **traditions**, and **meaning**. By celebrating them, we **connect** to our **past**, our **community**, and our **values**. And most of all, we get to **come closer** to **God** and the people we love.

So, are you ready for the next Holiday

Sabbath and Its Rituals

Do you know what makes **Friday evening** and **Saturday** so **special** for many Jewish families around the world? It's the **Sabbath**, or **Shabbat**, a **day** for **resting** and **celebrating**. It reminds us of the **seventh day** when **God** took a **break** after **creating** the **world**. Think of Shabbat as a **weekly timeout**, a chance to put everyday work on hold and **focus** on **family**, **friends**, and spending time together.

The **Shabbat celebration** starts on **Friday evening** when the **sun goes down**. In every Jewish home, two special candles are lit, symbols of the light and peace that Shabbat brings. You might wonder, why two candles and not just one? Each candle stands for one of the Torah's commands: "remember" and "observe" the Shabbat. When these candles are lit, a special blessing is said, and that's the signal that Shabbat has started.

After this ceremony, it's time for a **festive meal**. Picture a **big table** loaded with yummy **foods**, featuring **challah**, a special braided bread. Why is it braided, you ask? Well, the **braids** stand for **love** and **unity**, important values that Shabbat helps us celebrate. Wine or grape juice is also served and blessed, reminding us of life's sweet moments.

Then, it's **Shabbat** day. A day to **rest** and **enjoy** time with **family**. You might think it's boring not to play video games or watch TV, but actually, there's so much to do on Shabbat. You can read your favorite book, play board games with your family, go for a walk outside, and admire nature's beauty. It's a day to **appreciate** the **simple things** in **life**.

Prayer is also a **big part** of Shabbat. Many Jewish people go to the **synagogue** on Saturday morning to **pray together**. During this service, a portion of the **Torah** is **read** and beautiful **songs** are **sung** in honor of **Shabbat**.

Finally, when stars appear in the sky on **Saturday evening**, it's time to say **goodbye** to **Shabbat** with a ceremony called **Havdalah**. A scented **candle** is lit, special **prayers** are said, and songs are **sung** to say thank you for the past Shabbat and **get ready** for the **week ahead**.

So, **Shabbat** is **much** more than just a **day off**. It's a chance to **reconnect** with **family**, **celebrate life**, and **appreciate** what we **have**. So, the next time Friday evening rolls around, you can think about Shabbat and all it means. And now, a little question for you:

What's your favorite **Shabbat** tradition you learned about today ?

Kosher Food

So, have you ever heard the word "**kosher**"? It sounds a bit **mysterious**, doesn't it? Well, don't worry, we're going to unwrap it all together! In Judaism, "**kosher**" is a word that means "**clean**" or "**fit**." And when we talk about **food**, **kosher foods** are those that are **allowed** to be **eaten** according to **Jewish laws**. You might be wondering why we have these rules? Well, they have **spiritual** and **symbolic meaning** for us, and they also remind us of the importance of **taking care** of our **health**.

Now, you're probably wondering **which animals** are **kosher**? Well, we have **pretty strict rules** for that. **Animals** that **chew** their cud and have **split hooves** are considered **kosher**. That means we can eat animals like cows and sheep, but not pigs, because they don't have both these features. **Fish** must have **scales** and **fins** to be kosher. That means yes to salmon and tuna, but no to shellfish like crabs or lobsters.

And it's not just the type of animal that matters, but also **how** it is **slaughtered**. For an animal to be kosher, it has to be killed in a very specific way, in a manner that causes the **least suffering** possible to the **animal**. This is called kosher slaughtering. You see, in Judaism, we care a lot about the well-being of animals and think it's important to treat them with **respect** and **kindness**.

Now, remember when I told you that certain things **can't be eaten together**? Well, one important rule is that we **don't eat meat** and **dairy products together**. That's because we want to **separate life**, symbolized by **milk**, from **death**, symbolized by **meat**. It's a way of showing our **respect** for life.

All these **rules** might seem a bit **complicated** to you, but they are actually very **important** to us. They remind us of our connection with **God** and our **Jewish values**. By following these rules, we show our **commitment** to our **faith**.

Kosher food not only connects us to God but also to our **history** and **heritage**. When we eat special foods on holidays like Passover, we remember the history of our people. It's a way to feel **connected** to all the **generations** of **Jews** who came before us.

Today, **choosing** to eat **kosher** is a way for many Jews to **live** their **faith** and feel **connected** to their **community**. It's a **personal choice** that each Jew can make. And by choosing kosher foods, they can be sure that their food has been prepared **ethically** and **responsibly**.

So there you have it, **now you know** what **kosher food is**! While not everyone follows these rules, they are an **important** part of what it **means** to be **Jewish** for many people.

And don't forget, even though these rules may seem complicated, they're all based on the idea of being **kind**, **respecting life**, and **taking care** of our **world**. These are things that everyone, Jewish or not, can understand and appreciate.

Prayer and Synagogues

As you already know, **prayer** is a very **important practice** for us Jews. It helps us **talk** to **God**, tell Him how we're **feeling**, and **get closer** to **Him**. You know how you say hello to your friend when you see them? Well, prayer is like saying hello to God, telling Him about your day, and thanking Him for everything He gives us.

And when do we talk to God? We do it **three times** a **day**: in the **morning** when we wake up, in the **afternoon**, and at **night** before we go to sleep. We also have **special times** to pray during **holidays**. It's like having a very important meeting with a very special friend!

Most of the time, we say these **prayers** in a **place** called a **synagogue**. Imagine a large room filled with beautiful decorations and happy people coming together. **Synagogues** are like our **special homes** for **prayer**. But that's not all! In the synagogue, we also gather to **learn** together, talk about our **stories**, and even **share** good meals.

You might be wondering **how** we **pray**? For that, we use special words in **Hebrew**, which is a very **ancient** and **beautiful language**. We also use special objects during prayer, like the **Talit**, which is a **large shawl** we put over our shoulders, and **Tefillin**, which are small boxes that we tie to our arm and head. These objects have very **special meanings** and remind us of our promise to do our best to be good people.

There are many **different prayers**, each with a **special reason**. Some prayers are even **sung**, creating a very **joyful** atmosphere. Children start **learning** to **pray** when they are very young, just like when you started learning to read and write. And you know what? You're encouraged to join in on all these prayers!

Prayer is a very special **way** to **feel close** to **God** and all the **people around us**. You can **think** of prayer as a **rainbow bridge connecting us** to **God** and our **beautiful community**.

So, are you ready to cross that rainbow bridge with us?

JEWISH VALUES

Importance of Study and Learning

Do you know how important **learning** and **studying** are in **Judaism**? It's so essential that we could almost say it's the **heart** of our **religion**. In fact, our sacred texts like the Torah and the Talmud are like a **big treasure map**. This map helps us **understand how** to **live**, what is right and good, and how to **get closer** to **God**.

These **texts** are full of **wisdom**, **stories**, and life **lessons**. Just imagine! It's like having an adventure book that also guides you in life. And that's not all, we believe that **studying** these texts is a form of **prayer**. Yes, you heard right, a form of prayer! So when we read these texts, we often ask God to help us understand and interpret what we're reading.

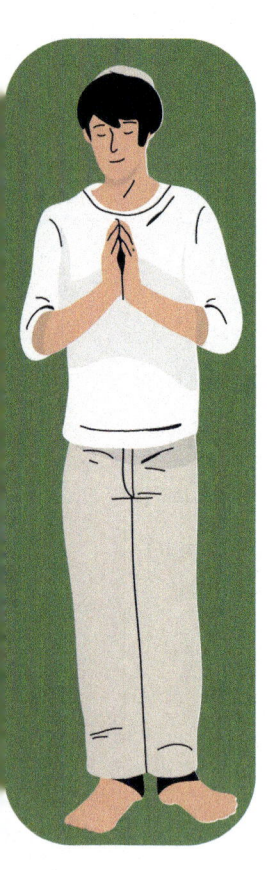

Now, you might be wondering **where** we **learn** all these things? Well, we have **special schools** for that, called **yeshivot** and **kollels**. These are places where we can study together, deepen our understanding and knowledge of Judaism.

And what about the children? Well, **religious education** is **very important** for Jewish kids. Jewish schools teach the Torah and other sacred texts, as well as the practices and values of Judaism. Can you believe it? It's like going to school, but in addition, you get to learn about your **religion** and **culture**.

And do you know what **language** all these **sacred texts** are written in? It's **Hebrew**, the **traditional language** of the **Jewish people**. So learning Hebrew is also very important; it's like holding the key that opens the treasure of these texts!

שבת
שלום

In the end, **study** and **learning** are **pillars** of **Judaism**. They help us better **understand God**, live according to our **values**, and **grow** as people. And you know what? By constantly learning and staying curious about the world around us, we can become **better** members of our **community** and even make a **positive** difference in the world.

Charity and Kindness Toward Others

Do you remember the superpower we talked about, the one of **kindness**? Well, in **Judaism**, this power has special **importance**. We call it "**charity**," but it's not just about giving money. It's also about giving your **time**, **love**, **patience**. It's about **helping others** feel better.

Think about all the times you've **helped someone**: maybe you've helped a friend **carry** a heavy bag, or **given** a slice of your snack to someone who forgot theirs? That's what **charity** is. And there are so many ways to express it. You can help at **home**, volunteer in your **community**, or simply offer a **smile** to someone in need.

But do you know why it's so important? Because **every time** you show **charity**, you **become** a **kindness superhero**. You **help** not only **others but** also build **yourself** into becoming a **better** person.

Never forget to be **kind** and **compassionate** to **everyone** you **meet**. You never know what someone is going through, so always be ready to offer your superpower of kindness, no matter who you're dealing with.

Respecting Parents and Elders

In Judaism, it's **really important** to **respect** your **parents** and **older people**. You might be wondering why? Well, they've lived longer than you, they've **learned** a **lot** of things, and they have tons of **wisdom** to **share**. By **respecting** them, you can **learn** a lot from them!

So, **how** can you **show respect** to your parents and elders? There are lots of ways! You can **listen** to them when they **talk**, **help** them when they **need** help, and **show** them that you **care** about them. For example, you could help your parents with the dishes, or offer to help your grandma carry her grocery bags. These are **small things**, but they show that you **respect** and **appreciate** them.

In Judaism, there are also special holidays that help us show our **respect** for our **parents** and **elders**. One of them is **Purim**, a joyful holiday where we give **gifts** to our **loved ones** and **older people** in our **community**. It's a beautiful way to show them how much we **love** and **respect** them.

Shabbat is another really special time. Every week, the family comes together to share a meal and pray together. It's a time to **get closer**, to **learn** from your **parents** and **grandparents**, and to share the values and traditions of Judaism. By **honoring Shabbat**, you also show your **respect** for your **family** and **community**.

Shabbat Shalom

Respecting your **parents** and **elders** is more than just a tradition; it's a **skill** that will be **useful** to you all your life. By **learning** to **respect** others, you **learn** how to **build harmonious** and **enriching relationships**. And who knows? One day, you might be the one sharing your wisdom with the younger ones!

Justice and Peace in the World

You know, in our religion, **two big values** are really important: **justice** and **peace**. What does that mean? Well, justice is all about **always trying** to do what's **fair** and **right**, whether it's with your friends at school, with your parents at home, or even with people you don't know. For example, if you see someone being treated unfairly, you can **stand up** and say that's **not right**. Or if you have two candies, you can share them **equally** with your brother or sister. That's **justice**!

As for **peace**, it's a big **dream** we all have. We'd love to **live** in a **world** where **everyone gets along**, where there's **no war** or **conflict**. You know, peace isn't just the absence of war. It's also the presence of **respect**, **understanding**, and love between people. For example, you can contribute to peace by helping to **resolve** a **conflict** between your friends, or by **learning** to better understand people who are **different** from you.

And guess what? Every time **you** act **justly** or work for **peace**, you **help** make our **world** a **better place**. Every **little action** counts, and we can all do our **part** to **build** a more **just** and **peaceful world**. So, never forget: always be fair, and work for peace. Together, **we can make a big difference!**

GAMES & ACTIVITIES

Now, Let the Games Begin !

What an **amazing adventure** we've been on together so far! We've traveled through **history**, met **captivating personalities**, and **explored traditions** that give **Judaism** its **unique richness**.

But now, it's time to **relax** and **have fun**! In this section, we've cooked up for you a series of **exciting games** and **activities** that will let you **test** your newfound **knowledge**. And feel free to **invite** your **parents**, **siblings**, or **friends** to **join** you. It's even more entertaining when played as a **team**!

So, grab a **pencil**, make sure you're comfortably seated, and get ready for **quizzes**, **riddles**, and even **word games**! Everything is designed for you to have fun while reinforcing what you've learned.

Are you ready to take on the challenge ?

If so, let the **games begin!**

Hidden Words of Judaism

Can you find the **hidden words** in this letter **grid**? Be careful, they can be **vertical** or **horizontal**!

Y	O	M	K	I	P	P	U	R	R	G
K	H	Y	C	H	A	R	I	T	Y	H
A	E	M	H	A	N	U	K	K	A	H
B	D	E	K	O	S	H	E	R	Z	Y
S	T	N	M	O	S	E	S	F	K	F
A	T	O	X	K	A	L	P	N	M	W
B	O	R	Y	G	O	L	I	A	T	H
B	R	A	L	A	A	L	I	Y	A	H
A	A	H	S	H	O	F	A	R	X	K
T	H	P	A	E	I	C	T	T	R	I
H	H	P	I	S	R	A	E	L	A	E

If you need a **little hint**, the **solutions** to the games are at the **end** of the book!

QUIZ

MULTIPLE CHOICE

Think you know everything about Judaism?

Put your **knowledge** to the **test** with this captivating **quiz**! For each question, you'll have **three** answer choices. Pick **the one** that seems most accurate to you.

The answers are at the end of the book, but try to answer first without looking, okay?

1. WHO IS CONSIDERED THE FATHER OF THE JEWISH PEOPLE?

A. ABRAHAM
B. MOSES
C. DAVID

2. WHICH HOLIDAY CELEBRATES THE LIBERATION OF THE JEWS FROM EGYPT?

A. PASSOVER
B. SHAVUOT
C. ROSH HASHANAH

3. WHAT IS THE ORIGINAL LANGUAGE OF THE TORAH?

A. HEBREW

B. ARAMAIC

C. YIDDISH

4. WHAT IS THE MOVEMENT OF RETURN TO ISRAEL CALLED?

A. DIASPORA

B. ALIYAH

C. HASBARA

5. HOW MANY DAYS DOES THE PASSOVER HOLIDAY LAST?

A. 1 DAY

B. 8 DAYS

C. 12 DAYS

6. WHAT IS THE WEEKLY DAY OF REST IN JUDAISM?

A. ROSH HASHANAH
B. SHABBAT
C. HANUKKAH

7. WHAT IS THE MEAL THAT STARTS PASSOVER CALLED?

A. SEDER
B. SHABBAT
C. KIDDUSH

8. WHAT IS THE PLACE OF PRAYER CALLED?

A. SYNAGOGUE
B. TALIT
C. KOSHER

QUIZ
OIX MULTIPLES

9. WHAT DOES "KOSHER" MEAN?

A. ACCEPTABLE
B. FORBIDDEN
C. STRANGE

10. WHICH TEXT IS A RABBINIC WRITING?

A. BIBLE
B. TALMUD
C. KABBALAH

11. WHICH QUALITY IS HIGHLY VALUED IN JUDAISM?

A. HUMILITY
B. WEALTH
C. POPULARITY

Judaism Crossword

Use the clues provided to fill in the crossword grid.

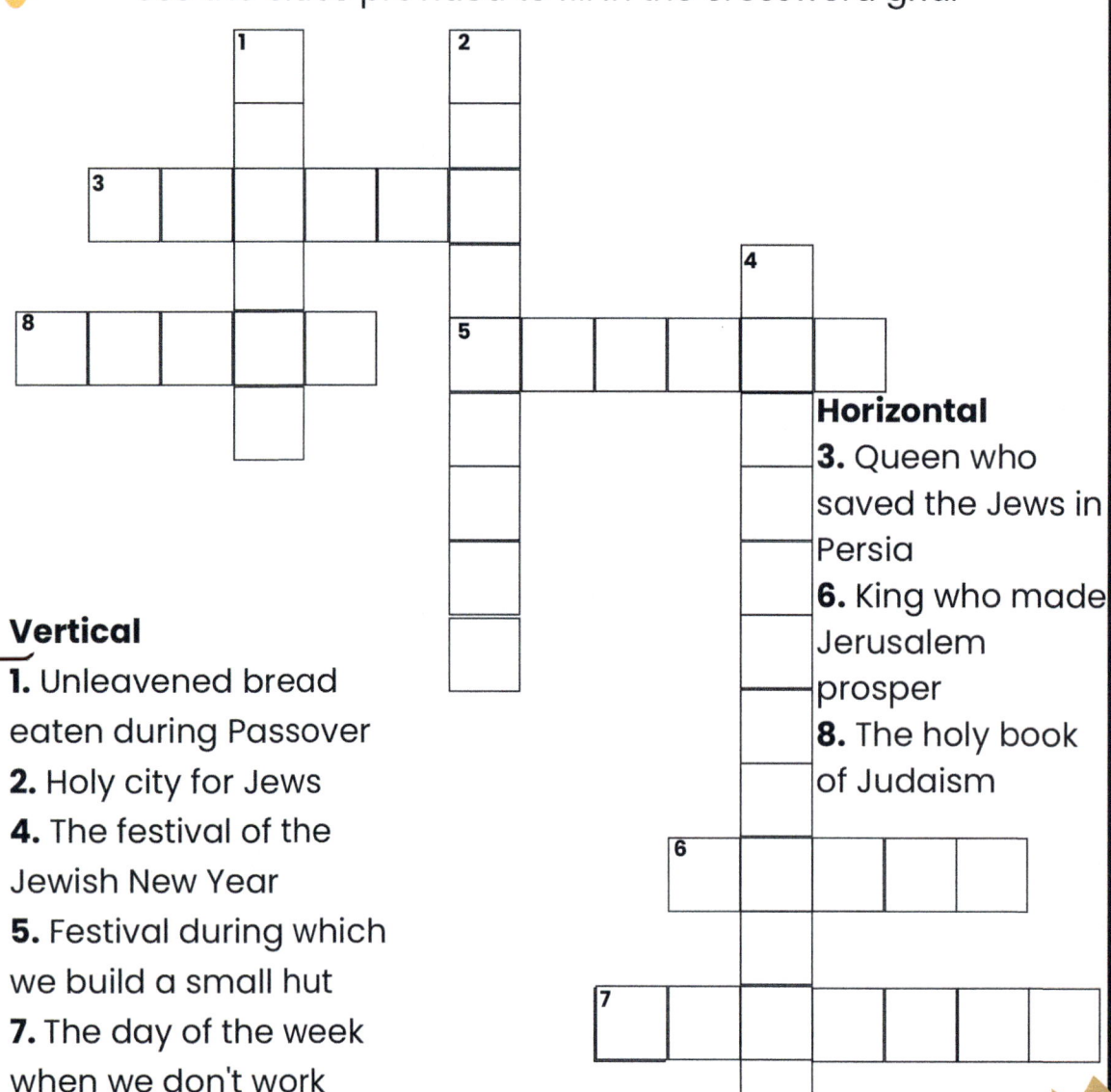

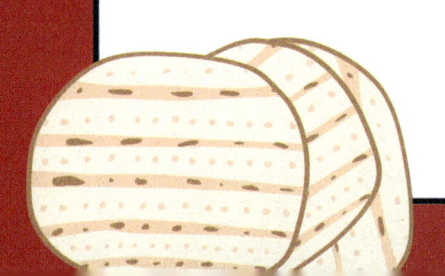

Horizontal
3. Queen who saved the Jews in Persia
6. King who made Jerusalem prosper
8. The holy book of Judaism

Vertical
1. Unleavened bread eaten during Passover
2. Holy city for Jews
4. The festival of the Jewish New Year
5. Festival during which we build a small hut
7. The day of the week when we don't work

Maze

Help this lost child **reach** the **synagogue** through this **maze** full of obstacles and detours!

Somes riddles...

What Do You Know About **Judaism**?
Answer the following **riddles**!

1 I'm braided and I'm on the Shabbat table, what am I?
_____
_____

2 How many times do Jews pray each day?
_____
_____

3 I am the symbolic foods eaten during Rosh Hashanah, what am I?
_____
_____

4 What are the two special objects used during prayers?
_____
_____

5 Term describing violent attacks against Jews?
_____
_____

6 Who led the Israelites (Jews) out of Egypt?
_____
_____

Match image to word

Match each picture with the correct word!

- Star of David
- Talit
- Shofar
- Menorah
- Torah
- Challah

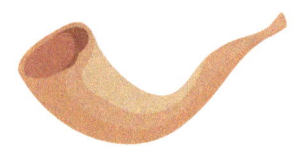

Coloring

Here are soms symbols and images associated with Judaism. Grab your crayons and bring them to life!

EASY

EASY

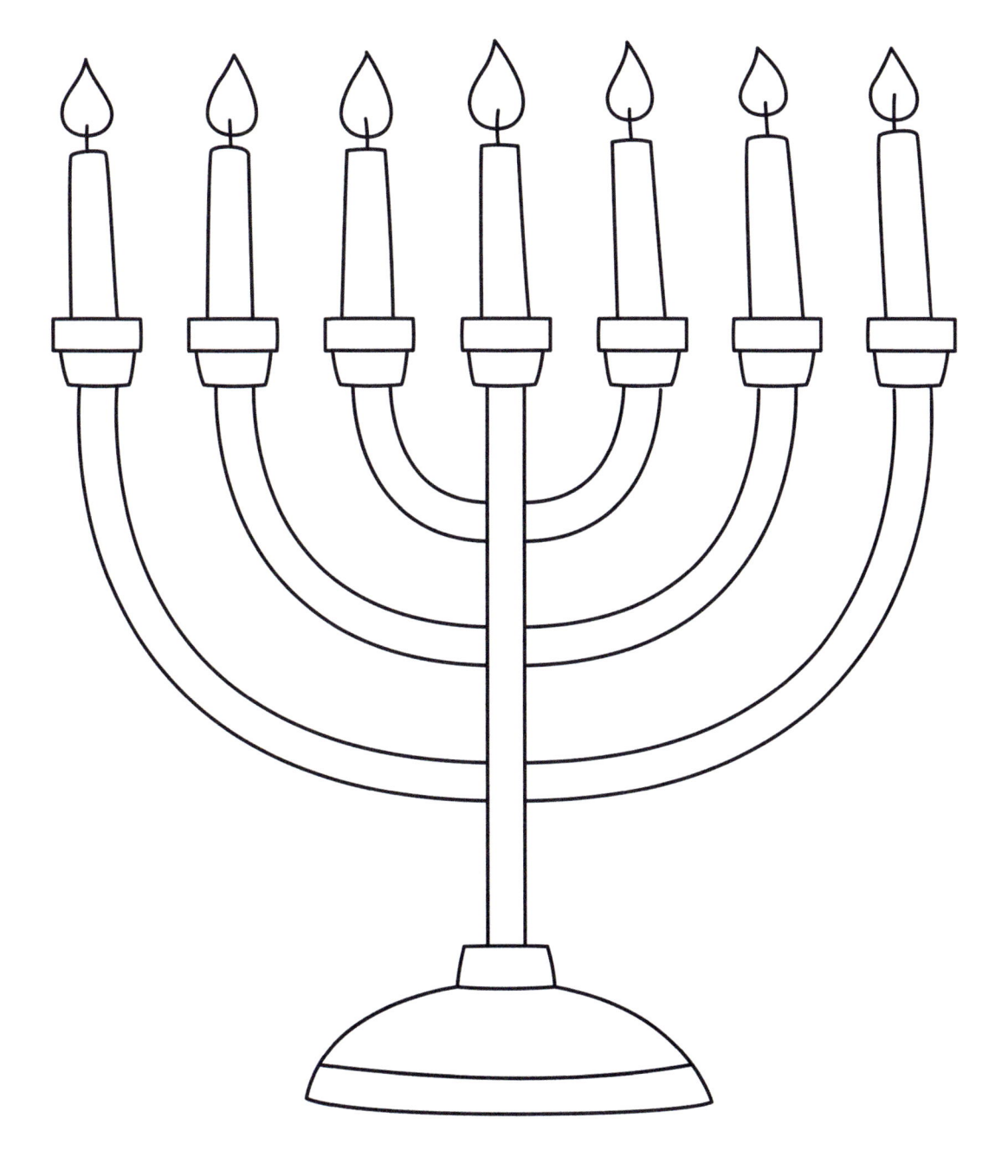

EASY

MEDIUM

MEDIUM

MEDIUM

HARD

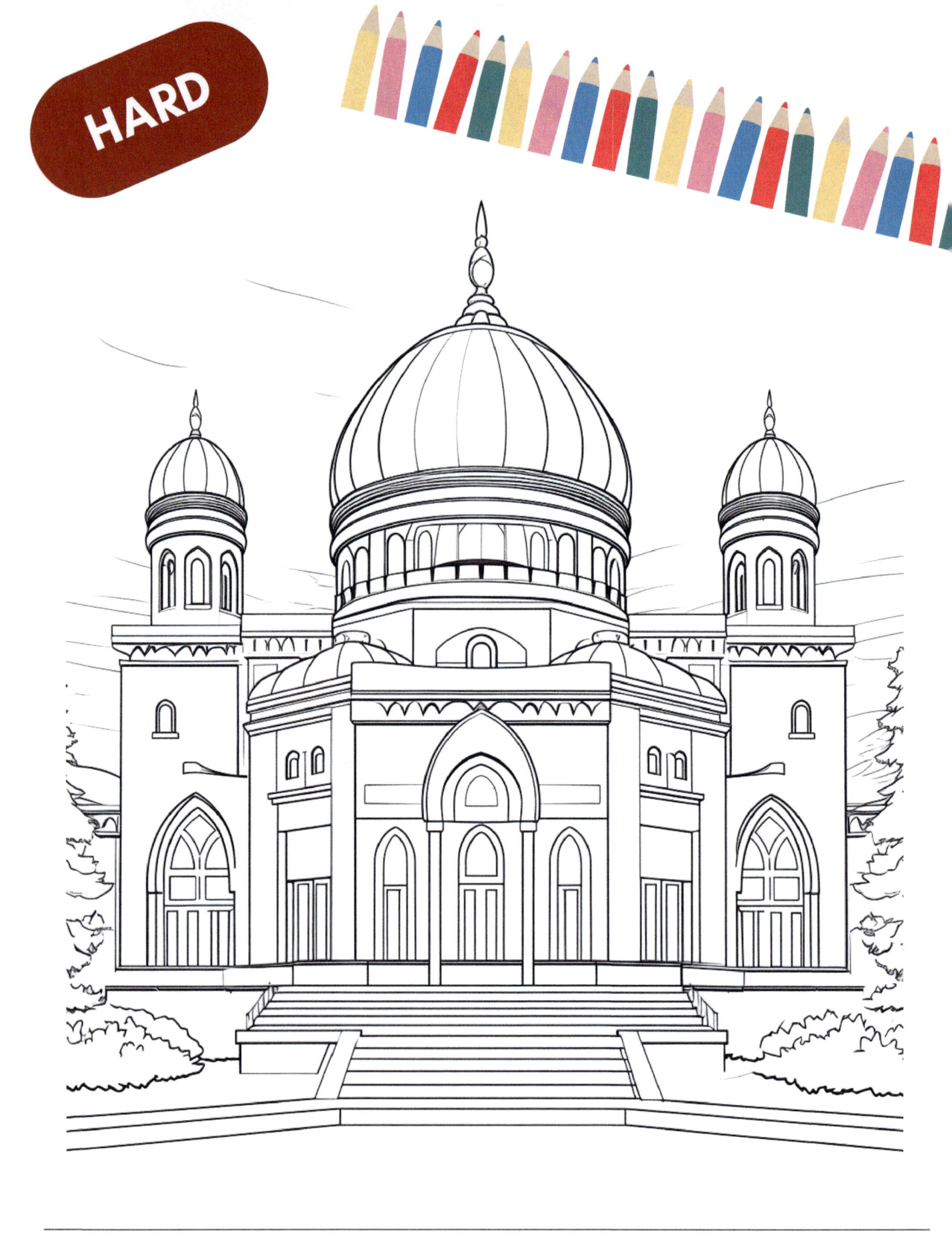

HARD

HARD

Solutions

Hidden words of Judaism

- Yom Kippur
- Charity
- Hanukkah
- Kosher
- Moses
- Goliath
- Aliyah
- Shofar
- Israel
- Sabbath
- Torah
- Menorah

Judaism Crosswords

- Word 1 : Matzah
- Word 2 : Jerusalem
- Word 3 : Esther
- Word 4 : Rosh Hashanah
- Word 5 : Sukkot
- Word 6 : David
- Word 7 : Shabbat
- Word 8 : Torah

QUIZ — MULTIPLE CHOICE

- Question 1 : Abraham
- Question 2 : Passover
- Question 3 : Hebrew
- Question 4 : Aliyah
- Question 5 : 8 days
- Question 6 : Shabbat
- Question 7 : Seder
- Question 8 : Synagogue
- Question 9 : Acceptable
- Question 10 : Talmud
- Question 11 : Humility

Some riddles...

- Riddle 1 : Challah
- Riddle 2 : 3 times
- Riddle 3 : Apple, honey & pomegranate
- Riddle 4 : Talit & Telifines
- Riddle 5 : Pogrom
- Riddle 6 : Moses

Match image to word

Challah — Torah

Star of David — Menorah — Talit — Shofar

65

SOME ACTIVITIES

CREATING A SEDER PLATE

As you've learned, the Seder is the ritual meal of Passover. You can create your own Seder plate by decorating a large plate or tray with the Seder elements, such as lamb, herbs, bread, and wine.

MAKING A MEZUZAH

A mezuzah is a small box containing a parchment with verses from the Torah. It is affixed to the doorframe of the home's entrance. You can make your own mezuzah by decorating a small wooden box and writing or drawing the appropriate verses on a parchment!

DECORATING HANUKKAH CANDLES

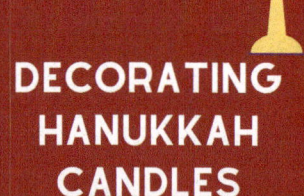

Hanukkah is the festival of lights. You can decorate candles with glitter, beads, and stickers, then light them each night of the festival to celebrate the Maccabees' victory and the rededication of the Temple in Jerusalem.

CHALLAH WORKSHOP

You can also make your own Challah for Shabbat! Mix flour, water, yeast, and a little oil. Knead, braid, and into the oven it goes! It's as simple as that (you can also ask an adult for help).

MAKING AN ISRAELI FLAG

You can make your own Israeli flag by drawing the Star of David on a piece of fabric or paper, then decorating it with the appropriate colors!

KEEPING A GRATITUDE JOURNAL

Grab a notebook and write down something that makes you happy or grateful each day. It's a great way to remind yourself of all the good things in life!

GLOSSARY

You've just journeyed through an **exciting exploration** of **Judaism** and its many facets. But don't put away this book just yet! This **last section** is the icing on the cake. The **glossary** you'll find here will allow you to **revisit** certain **terms** and **concepts** you've discovered throughout your reading. If a **word slipped** past you or if you wish to **deepen** your **understanding**, **now is the time!**

- **ALIYAH**: A Hebrew word meaning 'ascent.' It refers to the immigration of Jews from the diaspora to Israel.

- **BAR MITZVAH**: A ceremony marking a boy's coming of age and his responsibility before God, generally celebrated at the age of 13.

- **BAT MITZVAH**: A ceremony similar to the Bar Mitzvah, celebrated for girls at the age of 12 or 13.

- **CANAAN**: The land promised to Abraham and the Hebrews in the Hebrew Bible, which roughly corresponds to present-day Israel.

- **KOSHER**: A Hebrew word meaning 'fit' or 'proper.' It designates food and drinks that are in accordance with Jewish dietary laws.

- **HANUKKAH**: The Jewish holiday celebrating the Maccabees' victory over the Assyrians and the rededication of the Temple in Jerusalem.

- **MEZUZAH**: A scroll containing Torah excerpts, placed on the right-hand doorpost of a house.

- **PASSOVER**: The Jewish holiday commemorating the Jews' exodus from Egypt, marked by the consumption of matzah and the holding of the Seder.

- **POGROM**: A violent and deadly attack against a Jewish community, often perpetrated with the complicity of local authorities.

- **PURIM**: A Jewish holiday celebrating the Jews' victory over Haman, the advisor to the King of Persia who wanted to exterminate them. It's marked by the reading of the Megillah, the Book of Esther, and by costumes and gifts.

- **RABBI:** A religious leader in the Jewish community, an expert in Jewish law and traditions.

- **ROSH HASHANAH:** The Jewish New Year, marked by the blowing of the shofar and reflection on one's actions over the past year.

- **SHABBAT** : The weekly day of rest that starts on Friday evening and ends on Saturday evening. It is marked by prayers, family meals, and moments of relaxation.

- **SUKKOT**: A Jewish holiday commemorating the exodus from Egypt and the Hebrews' journey in the desert. It lasts seven days and is marked by the construction and decoration of a sukkah, a leafy hut, in which Jews take their meals.

- **SYNAGOGUE**: The place of worship where Jews gather for prayer and Torah study.

- **TALMUD**: A set of sacred texts in Judaism containing rabbis' commentary on the Torah, Jewish Law.

- **TEFILLIN**: Boxes containing Torah excerpts, worn on the head and left arm during the morning prayer.

- **TORAH**: The holy book of Judaism, containing the first five books of the Bible.

- **YOM KIPPUR**: The Day of Atonement, marked by fasting and prayer to ask for God's forgiveness

IN CONCLUSION

Congratulations!

You now have a **solid understanding** of the basics of **Judaism**. You've learned about the **origins of Judaism** and how it has **evolved** over **time**. You've discovered **key figures** in **Jewish history** and how the Jewish **people** have overcome difficult **challenges**.

Judaism isn't just **limited** to **practices**; it's also **founded** on essential **values**. You've learned how important **study** and **learning** are in this religion, as well as **charity**, **kindness** towards others, **respect** for parents and elders, and the pursuit of **justice** and **peace** in the world.

Lastly, we've provided **games**, **puzzles**, and **activities** to help you **review** everything you've **learned** while **having** fun at the same time. We hope this book has given you an **exciting** and **informative overview** of **Judaism**.

Now that you've **learned** the basics of **Judaism**, you're **ready** to **discover** even **more**! There are numerous books, websites, films, and museums that will allow you to deepen your **understanding** of this rich and fascinating **religion**.

For example, you could **visit** a **synagogue** near you to attend a ceremony or participate in a Jewish holiday. You can also **read books** about key figures in Jewish history or the different branches of Judaism.

If you're **eager** to discover the history of the Jewish people, consider **visiting** The Jewish Museum in **New York City** or the United States Holocaust Memorial Museum in **Washington, D.C**. if you're in the USA. For those in the UK, you might want to check out The Jewish Museum **London** or the Holocaust Exhibition at the Imperial War Museum.

Don't hesitate to **ask questions** to your **parents**, **family** members, Jewish **friends**, or **teachers** to learn more about this exciting religion and culture. Judaism has so much to teach us about **tolerance**, **peace**, and **brotherhood**, so keep exploring and learning!

See you next time, young explorer!

DEAR PARENTS,

A LITTLE GIFT AWAITS YOU!
SCAN THIS QR CODE TO ACCESS ADDITIONAL COLORING PAGES THAT WILL COMPLEMENT THIS EDUCATIONAL JOURNEY INTO THE WORLD OF JUDAISM.

YOUR CHILD IS GOING TO LOVE IT!

YOUR **FEEDBACK MATTERS** TO US!
FEEL FREE TO LEAVE A COMMENT ON OUR
AMAZON PAGE.
THANK YOU FOR BEING A LIGHT IN OUR PROJECT!

Printed in Great Britain
by Amazon